SECRETS OF
SOUTHERN DESIGN

———◆———

KIMBERLY GRIGG,
PRINCIPLE DESIGNER AND CEO,
KNOTTING HILL INTERIORS

Photographs by Carl Kerridge. Additional photographs by Matt Silk, as noted.

ISBN: 978-0-692-02054-8

Library of Congress Control Number: 2013951098

Printed in the United States of America.

For my very southern husband,
Roger, who has complete faith in me
but still bet me I wouldn't ever
get this book off the ground!

ACKNOWLEDGMENTS

Taking an idea from concept to book worthy is no small feat and like many things, it took a small village. The village soon became more like family, and it is with a warm heart that I want to recognize the following people with a great big thank you... thank you...

...To the hundreds of clients, shoppers, and attendees at my talks and seminars who have asked the questions, "How do you do this?" "What is right for my space?" "How can I make my home more beautiful, yet comfortable?" "How do you know how to arrange things this way?" "How can I get my husband to realize decorating is important?" and on and on...this is the true inspiration behind this book.

Additionally, I am grateful to...

...Carl Kerridge, my photographer, who is relentless in capturing the same visual details that I try so hard to present. You just seemed to "get me" and my message. Your patience, energy and artistry make this photo driven book a pleasure to put out into the world.

...My faithful and dedicated staff designer, Julie Schettig, you are my rock! We have worked so closely that we don't even have to use words to convey our ideas. Now this is truly a rare blessing! And to the rest of the Knotting Hill Interior's team, you work endlessly so that we have good content to share. I appreciate your dedication.

...Summer Turner, for teaching me the value of freewrites, for the endless edits, for cataloging and filing all these notes since we know that filing is not my strong suit, for the nudge to the finish line when I couldn't even conceive of what this meant and for sharing my vision of what this book should embrace. You have been an enthusiastic cheerleader and a joy to work with.

...The owners of all of the homes that we have invaded! Thank you for opening your doors and welcoming us into your homes, not only to decorate, but to photograph; yours is a hard job!

...My many clients over the years who have taught me how to work it out and make your spaces inviting and livable, all while maintaining peacefulness among the family members.

...My ever loving, abundantly supportive husband. You inspire me just by being you! Thank you for believing in me and for putting your loving arms around me after many long hours at the computer trying to manifest this dream. I appreciate your patience and your nudge!

...My wonderful children for being my cheering squad and for simply saying over and over by words and example, "You can do it...you can do it...you can do it..."

...To each of you...thank you for reading!

CONTENTS

Southern Man Spaces
Page 101

Southern Details
Page 119

CONTENTS

FOREWORD

Meeting Kimberly Gregg is like an exciting burst of intense color! As one of this decade's top Southern designers, Kimberly is energetic, delightful, and has an unparalleled exuberance for design. Her extensive knowledge coupled with her "call it like you see it" approach to her projects is refreshing and appreciated. When writing her blogs she leaves no stone unturned when thinking about design issues and solutions! Thus began my friendship with Kimberly, who I happily call my "color sister."

Kimberly has a unique way of pulling elements together to create exciting, rich interiors. Additionally, she adds bold color and layers textures with unexpected elements. Her designs provide elegant yet comfortable interiors that reflect her clients' taste and personality. She is funny, fabulous and a joy to know professionally—and it is a joy to follow her work! Enjoy!

Carolyn Hultman, ASID Allied

Carolyn Hultman Interior Design
Savannah, Georgia
Designer for Paula Deen

INTRODUCTION

You've heard of "southern hospitality" and "southern charm." They are real, ya'll. I grew up in the textile town of Graniteville, South Carolina, where I learned what being southern is all about.

Being southern is more than sweet tea and "blessin' yer heart." It's about manners and the art of gentility without stuffiness. This is a lifelong practice that begins by cultivating that part of you that genuinely wants to make other people feel good about themselves, which in turn makes them feel good about you. It is having a warmth toward life that is contagious; others feel it and want to be near it. We are not staid or stiff in any way. We are all about wearing our pearls and our flip flops at the same time.

Southerners are complex people and not so easy to read. We are not to be taken lightly. Like onions, we are made of many layers! We say grace before our meals and use the word darlin' whenever possible. We care deeply about our heritage. From the time we are knee high to a grasshopper, we are taught to have manners, saying "Yes Sir" and "Yes Ma'am." Whether talking to our mother, the waiter at a restaurant, our pastor, or girlfriends—we southerners treat everyone with equal kindness and respect.

We are taught to be gracious and hospitable, even when something happens that doesn't suit our fancy. Often you'll hear a southern woman resort to a stock saying such as, "Bless yer little 'ole heart." This can mean that she is empathizing with your situation or she is masking her true feelings and expressing her disapproval.

Southerners are colorful people. For our homes, we tend to gravitate to the warmer palettes to express the genuine warmth that is part of our culture. By nature, southerners are also gardeners. We love plants and tend to surround ourselves with beautiful foliage. Flowers from our gardens add another colorful layer of hospitality in our homes.

And, like a long, tall drink of lemonade on a hot day, southerners are there to give you aid and comfort in times of trouble. If a neighbor is ill or is experiencing a difficult time, a true southerner is going to show up at the door with both fresh flowers and a home-cooked meal.

To find out who a southerner really is, visit her home. For a southern woman, the home is a canvas for true self-expression. This is the case whether her home is a quintessentially southern historic mansion or something more modest. Right away, you'll feel the comfortable elegance and the genteel spirit—not too pushy and not overwhelming—that are the hallmarks of southern design.

Now sit back, put your feet up, and have a cup of tea in your finest china while I reveal to you the secrets of southern design.

Secrets of Southern Design

Chapter 1

A WARM SOUTHERN WELCOME!

We Southerners live at a leisurely pace, and sharing our hospitality with our family, friends, and the stranger within our gate is one of our greatest joys.

—Winifred G. Cheney
(author of *The Southern Hospitality Cookbook*)

Porches & Verandas

What makes southern design so special? Perhaps it is that the homes of southerners are gracious and graceful. To us there is dignity in beauty and elegance. Yet at heart we southerners are warm and friendly, so the design of our homes also reflects our need to roll out the endless welcome mat!

Inviting entryways, porches, furnishings that holler comfort, and personal collections are all ways that southerners extend their welcome mat. Southern design encompasses our need for expression and our desire to get to know you. When you walk into our homes, we want you to have a sense of who we are and also a sense of belonging in our living spaces.

The South for the most part enjoys a temperate climate, and so our porches—and those long, spacious, cooling-off porches known as verandas—are living spaces too! It is here that our famous southern hospitality begins.

In 2008 I was fortunate enough to be awarded the contract for the renovation of the world famous Pine Lakes Country Club in Myrtle Beach, South Carolina. Established in 1927, Pine Lakes Country Club is the most southern-inspired building in my town! Its back veranda is just about the most fabulous I've ever seen!

Here's a view of the front veranda—also impressive! In keeping with the classic exterior, my renovation of the interior was inspired by the Greenbrier Hotel, which iconic designer Dorothy Draper redid at the height of her career in 1949. I used Draper's book In the Pink *as an inspiration along with the movie* The Great Gatsby *to restore the club's original 1920s feel. (Perhaps the subject for a future book?)*

Spacious and gracious, this porch says, "May I please offer you a glass of iced tea?" Many a shared neighborly moment takes place on this back porch.

Ahh. . . can you feel the relaxation? Take a deep breath and sit and ponder. A mantle made from a tree that had to be cut down to accommodate the footprint of the new house; the warmth of a fireplace on cool days; a bench made of the same tree with the names of the children affectionately etched on it—this is what southerners are all about. The genteel spirit of the south: hard to define, impossible to pin down, and as flowing as the wind.

(Photos by: Matt Silk)

This client's foyer features a sweeping staircase combined with black walnut floors and heart of pine doors to create an air of genteel elegance. At the same time, it feels dressed down for a feeling of comfort. An antique slipper chair, with its perfect upholstery in very imperfect condition, helps create this dressed-down effect.

Foyers

People in the south are kind and genteel as well as charming and beguiling, and all these qualities are reflected in our homes. We want to let you peek inside our world by inviting you into our living spaces.

From the moment you walk in the door, you'll feel embraced by the sincere warmth of our welcome, no matter what the chosen design style. A southerner's foyer is thoughtfully designed and personalized to make you feel cordially received, to set the tone for what is to come, and to begin delighting you with an enchanting story about the people who live in the home. Look around to spot that touch of whimsy that reflects one of the many layers of the complex southern personality!

Notice the portraits of the children who live here appropriately added to the mix. Combining the old with the new is what makes this foyer come together with both charm and a certain freshness.

My new French-inspired foyer graciously welcomes you as soon as you enter.

Notice how a sizeable feature can look right at home in a space. Creating drama and impact, this large urn perfectly sets the tone in my foyer.

The foyer is one of the most important places in your home to feature personalized designs. Personalizing your foyer not only conveys a message to your guests; it also creates a renewed sense of belonging for you and your family whenever you come home. Wall paintings or murals are a unique and elegant way to tell a story about you and your family. As part of a recent renovation of my home's interior, I commissioned an artist to create a wall painting on my foyer walls and hallway. Reminiscent of a garden our family visited in France, my foyer constantly reminds us of a wonderful trip and a very happy time. Among the personalized details, such as our family dogs and a representation of my blue and white porcelain collection, is a tree containing leaves with the names of each member of my family!

My beloved standard poodle, Stella. Look closely and you'll see our tiny yorkie, Millie.

Perhaps you have a family crest. This can be prominently displayed in your own foyer via frame, or uniquely stenciled and painted as I did for my foyer's previous design. At a flea market, I had stumbled upon a book that included a crest and our last name GRIGG imprinted across it. I commissioned an artist to tweak the design and apply it to the foyer walls. Not only for guests but also for my large family of adopted, blended, and biological children, this wall treatment served as a subtle symbol of our identity and heritage.

Get Your "Southern" On!

On Your Porch
Reflect the refined yet relaxed welcome of the South on your front veranda and back porch. When you want to create that "grand" feel on your veranda, making your elements bigger does the trick!

On your back porch, create a lovely welcoming vignette of table, chairs, and potted plants that makes you want to spend time there, enjoying a refreshing glass of iced tea and a chat with friends.

In Your Foyer
Let your foyer begin telling the story of your family and what is to come in the rest of your home. Identify something personal and meaningful to you and your family, and incorporate it into your foyer design.

In the foyer of this client couple, a local artist hand painted elegant two-story trees, a meaningful symbol for this nature-loving couple. It's also a delightful, no-maintenance way to bring the outdoors inside!

Chapter 2

SOUTHERN COMFORT

"The single most important ingredient in a home is that it must have a soul."
— Charles Faudree (Interior Designer)

The soul of the southern home is grounded in graciousness and comfort. A southern home just wouldn't be southern if comfort was not fundamental to the design process.

Every person who walks into a southerner's home is made to feel like family right away. We might even say to you, "You're a sight for sore eyes!" We want you to gasp at the breathtaking beauty of our rooms and yet a minute later snuggle in as comfy as a kitten on the sofa. We want you to relax and put your feet up but also to serve you tea with our finest china.

However, comfort is not just about squashy down-filled cushions and butt-tested furnishings. It's also about carefully addressing the bones of the structure, as well as a furniture plan that allows for ample interaction both when you gather as a family and when you entertain. Comfort includes the way a room looks: a balance of light, texture, and color—with a touch of the unexpected.

What is the one big secret to creating successful southern rooms? Don't take yourself and your rooms too seriously! When all else fails and life gets too complicated, southerners begin to laugh! A sense of humor makes everything easier, and southern décor is no exception. When the room starts to feel stuffy, I'll add the unexpected or throw in something fun, like an unusual pillow or a chair that doesn't quite go. It releases the room (and you) from formality and offers a bit of casual elegance. Rooms need to feel like they are lived in, not just admired or respected from afar. When we let our hair down and allow our personality to show, our rooms will thank us for it!

Family Living Rooms

Strong use of color and functional seating arrangements help create cozy spaces that invite you to sit and stay awhile.

Both this photo and the previous one show a large great-room, which serves as a central hub for this young family. Two seating groups provide space for the children and guests to comingle either together or separately. Wallpaper is added to the coffered ceiling to create a dramatic effect.

Who says elegance can't also be "green"? The beams on this family room ceiling are made from reclaimed wood from an old barn. The table is made from rubber wood, which was fashioned into furniture once the tree's 60-year natural life span ended. In addition, throw pillows on the sofa were made from old rugs that were no longer usable.

(Photo by: Matt Silk)

In this family room, a large custom-designed cathedral ceiling is beamed to co-join the expansive space. To soften the effect, large-scale upholstered pieces are elegant yet casual enough to make you sit back, kick your feet up, and stay awhile. The unusual blend of colors, which are apple green, Wedgewood blue, and pops of coral, are both unexpected and soothing. I could live in this room forever! Couldn't you?

This living room is all about a beautiful gathering space. It is the central space of the floor plan, and as such I thought it would be fun to place a roundabout settee right in the center of the room. The ceilings in this room are very grand, yet the room is actually quite small. The furniture arrangement proved difficult, partly because the piano was a necessity. The roundabout ended up being the "important" piece in the room, as it provides extra seating while still contributing a certain "movement" to the room. This room has proven to function well for large gatherings (many of which I have been fortunate enough to attend), as the seating is perfect for groups or for more intimate conversations.

This living room expresses "southern comfort" at its best. The cool Benjamin Moore color "Pale Smoke" creates a restful atmosphere, yet there is a lovely juxtaposition of medium-toned wood furniture mixed eloquently with lighter tones. The luxurious overscale sectional with a chaise on the far end makes this sofa a pleasure to lounge on. The big fluffy chenille club chair in the foreground fairly screams "plop down!" The antique Oushak rug serves to warm up the space, yet it's also fabulous for disguising traffic wear and tear. Notice the wallpaper in the coffered ceilings—the icing on the cake that helps pull the whole look together.

(Photo by: Matt Silk)

This room captures true southern spirit in a traditional way. It features traditional colors and classic furniture pieces, but with a twist. A geometric pattern on the chairs and the zebra rug keep the room from becoming too serious.

(Photo by: Matt Silk)

This room expresses a combination of traditional and eclectic styles. A soft champagne neutral on the wall is punched up with hues of blue and bold dabs of red to create a room that is inviting and perfect for entertaining.

One of my favorite spaces in this client's home is the conservatory. It is light, airy, and oh, so restful. It was designed as a space for the homeowner to plant precious seedlings and then to relax with a perfect cup of tea!

(Photos by: Matt Silk)

It is important to me as a southern designer to always add the unexpected. I frequently do this with color. My staff often laughs when I say, "No, not that color—it's just too predictable. Instead let's spice it up and add something totally unexpected." This is where the artistry begins.

Notice the dramatic color on the wall. When you have a large space like this living room, intense color is desirable. It pulls the room together and makes it cohesive.

I used large-scale white porcelain flower plates to create art in my living room. This collection is unexpectedly placed directly beside an antique three-panel screen. The result is a fine blend of the old with the new. Voila! The room instantly becomes more interesting!

Southerners believe that making new friends yet keeping the old makes for a more interesting life. This applies in our homes, as well.

Kitchens, Dining Rooms & Breakfast Nooks

As we say in the South, the kitchen is the heart of the home. As southerners, we are taught from an early age to share our hospitality, and one of the ways we do this is with the expression of food. From fried chicken to casserole heaven—a southern table is just not complete without lots of food, home cooked with love.

Southern kitchens have evolved over time. Traditionally, southern floor plans have usually included a back door that filters right into the kitchen—where a neighbor can easily slip in for a quick visit. (If the kitchen table could talk, the stories would be unlimited!) These days, for some, the back door is gone and rerouted with a back entry that includes cubbies for today's busy family. The fact remains, however, that the southern kitchen is still a place that invites a free and open casualness—just like the heart of a southerner.

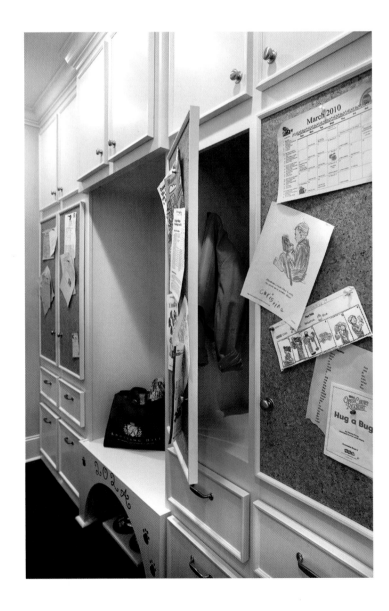

(Photo by: Matt Silk)

Ahh, the kitchen! This is the place where we southerners spend the most time (besides our beds!). Our kitchens are both livable and functional. They have to be, especially for southerners! For the kitchen in this French-inspired home in Myrtle Beach, South Carolina, I housed the sink in a lovely bistro chest that I commissioned to be handcrafted to resemble one I'd seen on a buying trip in France.

What I love most about this client's kitchen is the custom tile work as a backsplash for the stove.

This kitchen is not only comfortable, but lives well, too. A distressed table is the perfect surface for a busy young family.

This inviting yet highly functional kitchen was part of a whole-home renovation we did for a family that wanted to go "green." They even made a point to move back into their completed home on Earth Day. The table in the kitchen was made from reclaimed wood.

(Photo by: Matt Silk)

The highlight of the kitchen is this foot pedal sink. The man of the house is a doctor, and foot pedal sinks are common practice for him. These sanitary and water-conserving sinks are an easy and inexpensive upgrade. My clients enjoy the benefit of controlling the water flow, and their four daughters enjoy the sensation of "driving a car." The handles are for show, but the sprayer works— via foot pedals. This unique feature is high on the list of green recommendations and was a favorite during the 2010 Myrtle Beach Tour of Homes.

(Photos by: Matt Silk)

One of my clients received a massive collection of Mottahedeh blue and white "Canton" china as an inheritance from her mother. This collection became the inspiration for the whole house. Special consideration had to be given to the dining room, which is right off the foyer, because it is open to view from anywhere downstairs.

I am often invited into this home socially, and I love the feel of this room each and every time I visit. While it might be a bit fancy for some, it truly suits the style of the homeowners, who love to entertain. The monochromatic color scheme of "shades of blue" allows for a tranquil setting that is perfect for any occasion.

To accommodate this family's love of entertaining, I strategically designed the dining room for hosting guests at both casual and formal dinner parties. Sophistication and functionality were at the forefront of my mind when conceptualizing the layout, furnishings, artwork, and lighting. I specifically chose an antique three-pane display cabinet to complement the room's elongated oval dining table with Louis XIV-style straight-backed, armless chairs.

The dining table was shipped from Italy—we waited eight months for its arrival! I backed the chairs with a striped blue, cream, and soft-gold fabric to draw out the corresponding blue wall color, as well as the blue tones of the Mottahedeh art displayed in the cabinet. Reminiscent of the Parisian theme, I selected a bordered rug with detailed motifs and a short fringe in harmonizing hues.

This eat-in kitchen space is magnificent! A round table is a welcome addition to this breakfast area. Grouped with the interesting shape of the chairs upholstered in coral zebra fabric, this space says, "Come sit awhile and share with my family . . ."

Get Your "Southern" On!

What should no southern home be without? Comfort! A southern home without comfort is like a lamp without a shade! The key is knowing how to incorporate comfort into the home while maintaining a sense of elegance. And don't forget to add that little bit of personal whimsical charm that is oh, so southern! Here's how to achieve southern comfort in your family living spaces.

1. **Choose comfortable and well-constructed upholstery pieces, but dress them down by avoiding a matchy-matchy approach.** Mix it up: incorporate a blend of pieces—no "suites" of furnishings. Mix patterns on upholstery pieces that don't exactly match. This creates a down-home feel.

2. **Juxtapose the old with the new to create interest.** Bring in a fabulous antique piece (Southerners love tradition and heritage!) and surround it with other pieces that blend. Many southern rooms contain at least one good antique piece.

3. **Use warm, welcoming colors.** Stick to the warmer hues if possible. If you are using blues and some of the other cool tones, then use their warmer versions. You can always warm a cool color up by adding warmer tones as companions. For example, with blue walls, use warmer tones of greens for draperies. Add an unexpected color into the mix for a touch of whimsy.

4. **Use natural stones and woods on flooring.** Don't worry when the wood becomes worn. Southerners enjoy this look and refer to it as "patina'd."

5. **Personalize your living spaces with your collections or memorable accessories to show your individual personality.**

Chapter 3

SOUTHERN HERITAGE

"The South—where roots, place, family, and tradition are the essence of identity."
—Carl N. Degler (American Historian)

We southerners love our heritage! For us, it's all about history and a sense of story. It's about roots and where you come from. The antiques, memorabilia, and collections that often grace a southerner's home serve to express both our rich heritage and the personalities of the home's inhabitants. In other words, they show where we came from and who we are now.

Often rooms for southerners start with things handed down. They immediately bring an element of history into a room. They also offer guests an opportunity to connect with another layer of you, of your past or your ancestry. Incorporating these special and prized antique pieces in an artistic and modern way is fundamental to homes of the South.

Collections can be another fabulous way of preserving and showcasing memories. For many of my southern clients I suggest starting a collection for themselves—and also one for each of their children. While collections themselves are meaningful to southerners, displaying the collection artfully is also essential.

Antique Treasures

The antique sideboard in this dining room receives a breath of new life with a wonderful plate collection and beautiful modern but classic lamps. In keeping with the style of the sideboard, the chairs are made from reclaimed wood. We commissioned an artist to paint the birds and branches on the backs of these seats. I think they are magic!

(Photos by: Matt Silk)

A spiral staircase acquired from the burned ruins of a 15th century castle was retrofitted to meet current building codes.

(Photo by: Matt Silk)

Memorabilia

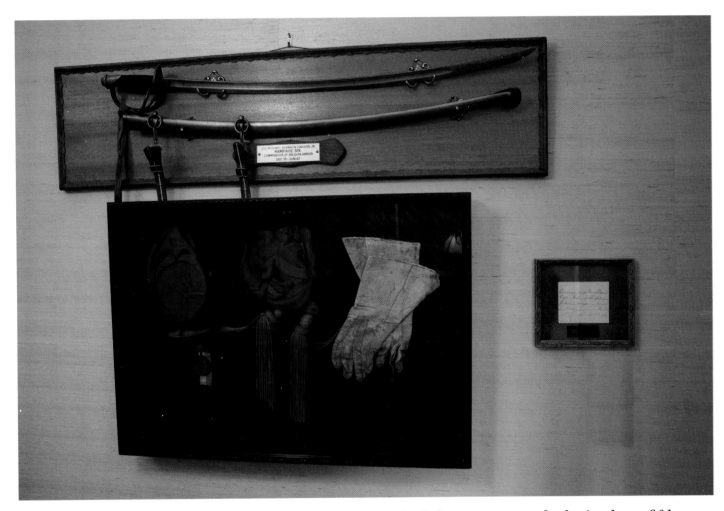

This foyer features a prized collection belonging to a retired three-star general who is also a fifth-generation West Point graduate. These family treasures include military awards, decorations, and memorabilia reflecting a prestigious military lineage that goes back to the Civil War. Here, some of the treasures are shown mounted in the foyer hallway.

A collection of family crests were attractively hung and displayed on the outside frame of the bookshelves.

To add interest in this master bath closet, we had the homeowners' favorite designer labels hand painted onto the closet walls. Both homeowners are clotheshorses, so this little detail really proved successful.

Personal Collections

One of my favorite collections is my own blue and white porcelain. I use it as a decorating staple throughout my home. The porcelain is also multi-functional: I have used many of the pieces to hold flowers from my garden, as well as to function as serving pieces for entertaining.

I started this collection when I was a child, hunting through junk fairs and discount stores. I've always loved to look at the various scenes and patterns on the porcelain pieces, which often tell a story. My collection today is much more varied both in quality and price but still includes many of those original pieces. This is the true beauty of blue and white porcelain. The price can vary, but each piece can still blend beautifully to make a lovely statement.

My beloved Staffordshire collection, which I had started collecting when I was pregnant with our last child, helps carry out the European theme in my home. There is strength in numbers, so if I have several smaller objects like this, I group them together for a harmonious impact.

Collections help us hold on to precious memories. My youngest daughter rides and shows hunter jumper horses almost every weekend, and each event produces anywhere from a few to a lot of ribbons. For a while I felt that our entire house was becoming overrun with ribbons. Frustrated, I put the ribbons in bags and basically hid them under the bed for two years!

Haunted by these ribbons, I had asked for display ideas in a blog post. While contemplating the wonderfully creative ideas I received, I stumbled across a white lacquered horse head on a buying trip to New York City. Here is what I came up with.

I had my upholsterer build a frame that would encase the lacquered horse head in a horseshoe shape. The frame was then upholstered in a green leopard print. Next, my sweet husband spent an entire weekend attaching string to the frame. The ribbons come with a clip on the back, so we just lined them up along the string.

The horse head sculpture display came out wonderfully and adds a great focal point to the room. Each of those ribbons represents an accomplishment, and I am so glad she is constantly reminded of how proud we are of her!

Monograms

Southerners love personalization! Monogramming is yet another means for expressing our sense of pride in who we are. Although in today's society we use modern monograms almost exclusively for aesthetic reasons, the history of monograms was more for identification purposes. In fact, monograms were first used on early forms of currency, such as clay coins, to indicate the ruler of each particular region. Royalty also used monograms to designate their valuable property, such as weapons and precious metals. Coats of arms were also an early example of monogramming.

Monograms were originally only two initials, whereas today we traditionally use three initials. This new format became popular in the 18th century. However, in today's society, the choice of what and how to monogram is completely a personal choice. Pretty much anything goes with monogramming, and we southerners take full advantage!

Notice the monogram displayed among the enormous amount of the porcelain on my dining room sideboard. My initial comes first, then G for Grigg is in the middle, and my husband's initial is third. This was once the centerpiece of my family photo wall, but I wanted to put it in a more visible spot and thought it was perfect over our dining room sideboard.

For these dining room chairs, I had the chair fronts covered in a velvet-like solid cream fabric with a customized silky-blue appliqué of the family's initials.

Get Your "Southern" On!

Southerners let their roots show! Display your family's handed-down treasures to showcase your heritage. Personalize your rooms by adding collections and objects that are important to you. Do it the southern way: relax and take your time. Comfortable southern interiors evolve. They don't look like all the stuff arrived on one day. Even when your home is professionally decorated, it should reflect a sense of who you are.

Chapter 4

SOUTHERN ROMANCE

"Romance is the glamour which turns the dust of everyday life into a golden haze."
—Elinor Glyn (1864-1943, Romance Writer)

Southern romance is alive and well! Courting is still in effect here in the South, and many southern homes still have a living room parlor which is used for that purpose. This may conjure up images of an antebellum South where a pretty belle in a voluminous gown and her dashing beau carry on a courtly ritual under the watchful eye of her family. Yet earlier in the day, that southern belle probably raced on horseback through soggy fields and enjoyed every mud-slinging mile.

Southerners are down to earth and as real as real can get. My youngest daughter once asked me, "How come you and Stella look so fancy, but out at the farm ya'll act just like Elly May Clampett?" Stella is our regal standard poodle, who is as elegant as the day is long. But when you let her loose out in the country, she turns into a sloppy, happy mess—a creature in love with life itself. At the end of the day, cleaned up and tired out, she's content to return to her elegant surroundings, where she fits right in, and dream of the day's delights. Stella perfectly illustrates the complexity of the southern way of being: down to earth authenticity right alongside Old World gentility.

My regal standard poodles Stella and Gatsby, who came along later. Both are beloved members of our large family.

The Master Bedroom

Southern bedrooms reflect the same qualities as those of true southerners. They are quiet, regal, and very elegant—yet down-to-earth practical, comfortable, and functional. We southerners like our bedrooms to include a bit of ceremony and a lot of pomp and circumstance. But when the covers are peeled back, we want this space to be the most comfortable room of all.

The bed is the heart and foundation of any bedroom, as well as the largest piece of furniture in the room, so it makes perfect sense to make it the focal point. In fact, most of the luxury of a bedroom can be achieved simply by focusing on the bed.

This bedroom is very large. Sometimes, believe it or not, it is more difficult to work with a too-large space than a too-small space. I filled the space adequately by hanging a very luxurious "crown" treatment over the bed, securing its prominence in the room. Next, I found a lovely old 12-foot-long French wardrobe. It is large in stature and provides three extra closet spaces for me. Finally, I filled the five banks of windows with full drapery treatment. I even have room for a sofa, in case one of my young ones can't make it through the night and needs a safe place to bunk.

Serene and tranquil, this southern bedroom is the quintessential perfect relaxing setting for a master suite. The miles and miles of silk used on the bedding speak volumes about luxury. A crown treatment along with a pair of French panels has this room wrapping its arms around you like a big embrace when you walk through the door. The adjoining sitting room provides a restful getaway. It coordinates beautifully as a companion to the master bedroom.

Perfect for reading or lounging, this seating area is hand painted like an open atrium. The result is soft, yet stunningly beautiful.

For this client couple, we found a Venetian crystal chandelier that commemorates his proposal of marriage to her on a bridge in Venice. What better place to install it than in the bedroom? Ah, southern romance! We also fully upholstered the walls, making this room very cozy indeed!

The Guest Room

Luxury, comfort, and *pampering* are all words I use to describe the perfect guest bedroom. Ever visited a lovely bed & breakfast place and left feeling lusciously indulged and lavished in the lap of luxury? Why not ensure that your houseguests leave feeling the same way? That's the southern way!

Many people make the mistake of putting all the leftover furniture they didn't use elsewhere in their home right in the guest bedroom. This only creates confusion, and somehow always comes off looking like a bad college dorm room.

A true southerner will give at least as much thoughtful consideration to the guestroom as to her own bedroom. She will begin with a pleasing color scheme that flows with the rest of the home, choosing soft, soothing colors, and adding lovely window treatments and artwork. Then she will add her own dose of personal thoughtfulness. She will always anticipate every possible need of her guests and provide those little touches that make her guests feel especially welcome.

Guests feel pampered in luxury in this guest room.

Sweet dreams!

Get Your "Southern" On!

Your Master Bedroom

Balancing a majestic regal look with comfort and functionality expresses the essence of southern romance in the bedroom. Here are a few hints to help you get your southern on:

1. For a soft, romantic mood, luxurious look, and cushy feel, choose carpets for your bedroom floor.

2. Decorate the bed. I often do this by adding bed canopies and draperies above the bed to create a crown affect.

3. **Pay attention to bedding details.** If I am using a bedspread, then I will still include a bed skirt, so that when the covers are pulled back the mattress is still covered. High quality sheets are a must, and loads of comfortable pillows complete the look.

4. **Take lighting seriously.** Lights on dimmers and lamps set on antique chests are lovely, but make sure that there is enough functional task lighting. Consider attractive swing arm lamps or a direct light at the bedside or over the bed to accommodate reading or a lazy day in bed doing crossword puzzles.

5. **Use beautiful boxes to contain the un-beautiful but necessary items we all want within arm's reach when we're in bed.** For example, tissue can be arranged in attractive containers on each side of the bed.

The Guest Room

Thoughtfulness is the key in creating a romantic southern sanctuary for your houseguests. Like a true southerner, you'll want to think of everything your guests might appreciate. Follow these tips and your guests will leave your home feeling nurtured and refreshed—and full of praise for your hospitality!

1. **Choose the right mattress.** Don't skimp here. Get a good mattress, preferably one with a built-in pillowtop cushion.

2. **Select the best bedding.** You might have thought that the higher the thread count, the better and softer the sheet. Not necessarily. Combed cotton is the best choice for sheets, and as long as it's 100% cotton, the thread count is not that important. For blankets, choosing a natural fiber such as cotton, wool, or cashmere makes under-bedding luxuriously complete.

3. **Make the bed the 5-star hotel way for true indulgence.** Start with a padded mattress cover followed by a fitted sheet. Then add the first sheet followed by a lightweight blanket and then a top sheet.

4. **For a touch of whimsy, borrow from the 5-star hotels and add small chocolates on a bedside tray.**

5. **Provide a cozy nook.** If space allows, add a chaise or chair and ottoman for a guest to curl up in for a good read or a nap. Don't forget a floor lamp to provide ample light. A soft fragrant wall plug-in air freshener (non-allergenic, of course) adds to the ambience.

6. **Add thoughtful touches.** Stock the room with flowers, a careful selection of books—don't forget a few pairs of reading glasses!—and a tray containing bottled water and a glass. Fill a large basket with bathroom luxuries: shower gels, special shampoos, and bath salts. Don't forget to include personal items that your guests might have forgotten, such as blow dryers, lotions, and a complete on-hand array of guest toothbrushes!

Chapter 5

SOUTHERN MAN SPACES

"Southern husbands are so simple! Give 'em not only good food but a comfortable chair in a space to call their own, let 'em think they're right and that you've stayed on budget—that says it all!"

—Kimberly Grigg (Southern Interior Designer)

The way to a southern man's heart is not only through his stomach but also through the comfort of his own chair in his very own man cave. I hate to admit it, but women have a way of making their spaces fit their own lifestyle dreams, and somehow a man's needs pale in comparison as she sets up the home to accommodate the needs of the family. As a wife and interior designer, I am all too aware of how my husband Roger's needs got pushed aside when we married and embarked on setting up our household.

The Man Cave

While Roger brought to the marriage a few significant pieces of English antique furniture, his "treasures" also included an oversize regulation pool table that really belonged in a pool hall, an assortment of deer heads and other hunting trophies, and a framed collection of every duck stamp known to humankind. With successful husband-wife negotiation, the pool table was sold and replaced with one more suitably sized for our home. But his hunting trophies and duck stamp collection just didn't fit into our French décor. I managed to relegate the duck stamp collection and some of the hunting trophies to his office.

At some point in our marriage, at Roger's request, I designed a shed for some equipment used for maintaining his hunting property out in the country. I also added a bunk room in case he ever wanted to stay overnight for early morning hunts. More of the hunting trophies moved out of my décor and into this shed.

Now, Roger has long since given up offering decorating tips and advice around our house, but he has remained steadfast about his comfort. Around the time that our sixth (and final) child was born, he announced that he needed a space of his own. He asked me to convert the equipment shed into a true man cave. I was elated because I could finally banish his remaining hunting trophies to this new site way out in the country!

From the outside, this shed appears to be just like any other metal shed, but the interior has the feeling of a small oasis in the woods.

Cabinets in a red glaze complement the commercial appliances and the rustic look. Countertops are made from the same stone as the fireplace.

There is a sleeping loft with extra bunks for the kids (whenever they are invited!). The bunks were made from trees on the property.

One of the challenges was to put together a space that doesn't feel decorated or contrived. In order to achieve this, I applied the basic rules of furniture placement and layout but kept the furnishings very organic. Antique farm tools are used as accessories. The dining table and chairs are made from trees from the property. The floor is stained concrete and is covered with a variety of old rugs, some of which are skins. Leathers, chenilles, and twills are paired with a plethora of animal trophies to create a great man's space that invites comfort.

As a weekend getaway, this space has met the challenge of creating and defining a getaway space where my man can spread out and be surrounded by his own things. It may not be a castle, but it is a place he can enjoy as a retreat any time he needs it!

Billiards Room

Lest I give the impression that I've banished my husband to the countryside, let me assure you he does have a "man space" in our home!

This is a "little man's cave"! It is a playroom area for my 12 year old son right outside of his bedroom that is perfect for lounging, watching TV and his extensive collection of sports trophies.

In the sitting and bar area of Roger's billiards room, I surrounded a round ottoman with four different chairs upholstered in the same fabric. It's so much easier to engage in conversation when you're seated "in the round." And nothing is more southern than this trendy arrangement, which says "welcome," yet is stately and elegant. While this room is definitely a man's preserve, it also is kid friendly and is a room in harmony with my French theme. It's a room I can live with.

Get Your "Southern" On!

Men like to retreat into their caves, surrounded by things that make them happy and comfortable. In all my decorating years, I have found very few women who want to be surrounded by masculine things such as deer heads. So I say if you have the space, give your man a room. If you don't have the space, find a way to make your man comfortable. Even if you have to give up some of your own space to accomplish this, in the long run you will be happier because he will be happier.

You also will have a place to put all those things that he brought into the marriage that he can't part with and you can't stand!

A client's "man room."

Let's get started. Find out:

1. Does your man want to be involved in the design process or does he just want to show up and enjoy the new space?

2. What things make your man happy? Is he interested in sports? Does he hunt? Does he shoot pool? Does he have trophies or collections? Does he watch television?

3. How will the room need to function? Will it need to serve as an office and lounging area? Office only? Does he like to entertain? Does the entertaining involve cards, sports, or something else?

Once you can assess this, then you can make your design specific. Keep in mind that this is one of those times when you might need the help of a professional. Rooms and possessions are very sacred to men (and we thought we were the sentimental ones!). Professional designers often can take the conflict out of this process or prevent one from occurring.

You should now know what furniture pieces need to be included and where they should be placed to create the spaces needed. In general, I find that men often want the following to be included in their space:

- Desk or somewhere to house his computer.

- File cabinet(s) or other storage pieces.

- Pool table or other sports-related apparatus (if space allows). By the way, don't underestimate how much space is required for a pool table. Many are 4 ft. × 8 ft. and will draw in nicely on a floor plan; however, you need a minimum of an additional 3 feet clear of any obstructions to comfortably shoot. Nothing angers a man more than to have things obstructing his ability to shoot—I learned this the hard way!

- TV and possibly several. Surround sound is not a necessity, but it is certainly desirable, and especially important for the sports fan.

- Comfortable furniture. I recommend that you NEVER buy a chair or sofa for your man without having him sit in it. I refer to this as the "butt test." I never select a chair or sofa that my husband is going to spend a lot of time in without having him butt test it. For my husband, some furniture causes him to lose circulation. Once you've narrowed down your search for the best chair or sofa candidate, have your man sit on it for a full 20 minutes. (I know, if you're doing this in a store they will probably want to charge you rent!) During that time, have him read a newspaper or whatever he normally does while sitting. After this, he should be able to tell if it is truly comfortable for him.

- Color. I find that there are a multitude of rich masculine colors that make men comfortable. In all my years of color specifying, I always find that men love blue—and almost any shade of it. Deep golds, browns, grays, and greens are also colors I find fairly universally accepted by the male population. When deciding on the foundation of the color scheme for your man, note his clothing color choices. Men are creatures of habit and tend to choose colors they feel comfortable wearing. If your man is a khaki and light blue button-down shirt kind of guy, those might be the best colors to surround him in!

• Memorabilia and collectibles. Encourage your man to be with the things he loves. If he is a hunter, hang his stuffed prey. If he is a fisherman, consider having some of his "plugs" shadowboxed. A golfer might want to own a collection of antique golf clubs. You get the gist. It's important to present not only who this man is but also to allow your man to be surrounded by the things that provide him with his greatest pleasure. And if those happen to be things you've been wanting to get rid of, well, mission accomplished!

• Door. Yes, I am serious—a door. Typically, men like their space to be their own, and I have found that they love the option of closing themselves off from the world or making themselves available only on their terms. By making sure that the room includes a door, I find that men enjoy feeling that they are truly the ruler of their own domain.

Now, I know that some of you women out there are going to feel tremendous resistance over the idea of giving up valuable real estate in your home just so your man can have his own space. Take it from me: I have seen countless marriages fester over the power struggles associated with how homes are decorated. My idea is to sincerely focus on making the man's space all he could ever wish for. When that is accomplished, just think of all the other spaces in the house that you now can rule in! It's a bit like that old saying: "Give up the battle and win the war."

Chapter 6

SOUTHERN DETAILS

"Beauty is an accumulation of details, the kind of layering that takes a long time."
—Hélène David-Weill (art collector and philanthropist)

While I have a degree in business with a strong emphasis in design, I most proudly possess a Ph.D. in details! It's the attention to detail that will make or break your style. It's in the details that you can put your own stamp on your home, and it's in the details that you can transform a house into a home. In a successful southern interior, personality triumphs over design.

Paying attention to the smallest of details is all part of a southerner's upbringing and training in hospitality. We truly care about our guests' experience in our homes. We want them to feel surrounded and embraced by the genteel elegance that characterizes the South, from our choice of wall color right down to the antique place card holders on the table.

Our attention to detail applies even in the most unexpected mundane situations. For example, at our house, a family meal is fun and elegant. A neighbor's child once told her mother that she loved to have dinner at Aunt Kimberly's house. The mother asked why and she replied, "Because she always lights the candles, even when we have paper plates!" Now that's elevating the everyday to a high art!

In a powder room that was destined to become the crowning jewel in a lovely home, we elevated its most necessary and functional fixture by adding unusual details.

This is the place where form meets function, and we all know that toilets are a necessity in any powder room. Finding the perfect toilet for this distinctive powder room proved to be a tall order. While searching high and low for the perfect toilet, inspiration hit me: a toilet chair! It was time to engage the services of my trim carpenter. By adding caning to disguise the base and back of the chair and by rebuilding a liftable seat, we achieved a result that is both unique and functional. We simply faux painted the entire chair to blend with the other components of the room. The effect is truly amazing!

Drapery Details

Beautiful fabrics, tassels and trim, and attention to details are a mainstay of good southern design. Historically, the South has been equated with textiles because many textile mills graced the region until textile production went overseas. Still, one of the greatest tools in the southern design bag is textiles.

How does a southerner use textiles in window treatments? There are many homes in the southern mix that contain very elegant swags and jabots, especially in the more formal rooms. Increasingly, however, homeowners seem to prefer a more modern mix of textiles.

I personally love classic drapery that doesn't have to be changed when the mood of a room changes. Drapery can be expensive, so I think it is best that it remain a constant in a home. It is easy to change paint colors, pillows, and accessories. It is a bit overwhelming to change draperies.

I persuaded my sweet husband to enclose our loggia so that it could become a family room that could accommodate all eight of us, plus our pets and neighborhood children. I painted the room a very bold green color.

I selected a bold floral pattern that would connect the indoors to the outdoors. My goal was to enhance the doors and windows, but not overpower them, while counterbalancing the power of the strong color. The juxtaposition of the soft floral with the strong color was just what the room needed.

Tablescape Details

There are endless ways to create the "still life" arrangements known as tablescapes, and they are not limited to dining room table centerpieces, as many people think. Southerners use every surface you can think of for tablescapes. After all, we have all those memorabilia to display! Layers of the right mix of old and new, traditional and quirky, serious and whimsical create a relaxed and casual yet sophisticated feeling that expresses the southern personality.

I use a symmetrical design approach when I want to achieve balance, harmony, and a bit of formality. For a more whimsical, informal look I'll go for an asymmetrical design.

A symmetrical tablescape.

An asymmetrical tablescape on a chest in a boy's bedroom. The shield on the wall helps to balance out the arrangement.

I often insert a carefully selected framed photo or two into my tablescapes. If I want to use numerous photos, then I select frames of a similar material and color. Collections can also be incorporated to create a unique tablescape.

Get Your "Southern" On!

Your Draperies

Drapery is fundamental to a well-dressed room. Over the years, designing wonderful southern spaces for my clients, I have discovered that nothing adds more polish and pizzazz to a room like draperies. And without them, the room seems unfinished and blank. As Cinderella once said, "One little shoe can change your life." The same holds true for one little magical window treatment.

The construction of window treatments is just as important as the fabrics and the design. First, it is important to consider the window and the view. Are we enhancing? If so, simpler is usually better. If we are creating an architectural detail, then "elaborate" may be in order. What feeling are you trying to create? This helps determine the direction of the design.

Attention to detail is key in creating window treatments worthy of a southern home. Here are a few tips to consider:

1. From a practical viewpoint, it is important to consider privacy concerns, as well as the amount of light that needs to be blocked. If privacy and light are a concern, then careful consideration will have to be given to whether the draperies will close, or whether or not a blind or shade of some sort can do the job.

2. A large-scale pattern is an ideal fabric choice for your drapes because they make a definitive statement about the room, yet the folds and pleats will keep the pattern from overwhelming the space.

3. **Line and interline your draperies.** For fabrics such as silks, I like to use what is known as English bump as the interlining. The bump is very thick and gives the fabric weight and body. Choose white or off-white for the lining, especially if it can be seen from outside. Lining and interlining draperies help the fabrics hang elegantly and properly while protecting them from sun damage.

4. **Consider the length of the draperies.** For southern elegance, I prefer full-length draperies that at least graze the floor, unless a window seat or cabinet interferes. Mount the treatment above the window approximately 2–3 inches below the crown molding or ceiling. Hanging your window treatments high above the window makes the window look longer, creating an elegant appearance.

5. **Use a professional installer.** My window treatment installer is to me like Murphy Brown's painter was to her! Installers are responsible for the overall final appearance of your window treatment. They not only hang all the components, anchoring the hardware properly for the long haul, but they also "dress down" the drapery, making it hang absolutely perfectly. Dressing down means that once the treatment is in place, the installer smoothes out all the wrinkles, makes the pleats even and crisp, and puddles the drapes. If you invest in custom interlined draperies, this dressing down step is critical to the success of your investment. So you can see that without a good installer who can "dress down" your draperies, they could end up looking sloppy.

Your Tablescapes

Creating beautiful and intriguing tablescapes on a variety of surfaces to wow my guests is one of my favorite things to do. Here are some things to keep in mind in creating your own tablescapes:

1. **First, choose the background.** Will a mirror hang over the piece? A work of art?

2. To create harmony, look for commonalities among the objects you're considering. A collection of items that relate to each other is far more exciting and will make more of a statement than individual, unrelated pieces arranged haphazardly.

3. Whether you create a symmetrical or asymmetrical design, you'll want to incorporate the principle of rhythm, which effectively blends all of the elements into one cohesive presentation.

   So, what exactly do I mean by a "rhythm"? If you look at a well-executed tablescape, you will see that it starts on one end with something high (such as a lamp or tall flower arrangement), tiers down to lower accessories in the center, and finally travels back up on the other end to taller objects. In a symmetrical arrangement, the taller anchoring objects will be the same height; in an asymmetrical arrangement, the final object will not be quite as tall as the first object.

If you use your hand to follow the motion of your well-constructed tablescape, you will see that it creates a wave-like movement, or a rhythm.

4. If you like to keep things simple, place a medium-sized object, such as a bowl of flowers or tureen, between two tall objects, and you're done!

5. If you use photographs in your tablescapes, then select frames of a similar material and color. They can be different sizes and then interspersed. One or two groupings of photographs is enough for any room; otherwise they become distracting and feel like a hodgepodge. In this case, less is more.

Details to Inspire You

I believe that any design style can reflect the comfortable elegance and the genteel spirit that are the hallmarks of southern design. The interiors featured in this section are from a client's home that is French-inspired—Parisian, to be exact. I think you'll be able to see how I incorporated the southern principles of hospitality, comfort, heritage, romance, and attention to details into these opulent, yet charming and definitely livable, interiors.

The dressing room

This dressing room is one of the most fun rooms I have ever decorated! When my client's husband agreed to turn the existing exercise room into a dressing room for his wife—especially since all of her clothing was already hanging from the treadmill and other sports equipment—I went, as we say in the South, straight to hog heaven! I was eager to dismantle the exercise equipment, haul it out, and bring a bit of glitz and glam into the space. The wall of exercise mirror was to remain. After all, what better way to start a dressing room than with an entire wall of mirror! To start making this room even more glam, I brought in a mirrored dresser and topped it with two very prissy lamps.

I situated a lovely antique settee and installed a large round custom-made jewelry chest with locking drawers to store the client's extensive jewelry collection. In addition, I found a lovely little French curio that houses even more jewelry. Its gold gild patina is beautiful and makes the jewelry look even more special. The chandelier takes the glam factor over the top! The shoe closet holds over 100 pairs of shoes. The adjacent closet contains hand-painted designer labels throughout.

My favorite detail is the lovely window treatment, which elegantly emerges from the balloon fabric wallpaper. The homeowners' initials are beautifully embroidered on coral silk that drapes over a lovely stripe. This window treatment brings all the colors of the room together in a subtle, charming, and refined way.

A small vanity table with a matching skirted seat was included to create the perfect spot for applying makeup. The round mirror is held in place by an embellished gold frame and helps tell the "Parisian story" of the dressing room.

The Study

In this study we debated whether to add cherry paneling to the entire room or to present a different option that would still have a strong masculine effect. I worried that the cherry paneling would enclose the room a bit too much and that the room, which is quite small, would become even smaller. My instinct was right, and once I discovered this "magic" fabric for the drapery, I knew I'd found the missing piece to the room. I immediately set about finding just the right window treatment design that would soften the existing cherry cabinetry yet provide an elegant but masculine detail. The fabric I chose said, "I am soft but important!" Next came the wallpaper detail. A handsome navy toile provided just the right background for the client's antique desk.

The Southern Way

They say that the South is the beauty queen of the nation. But no matter where you live—north, south, east, or west—you deserve to live in beautiful, elegant, comfortable surroundings that reflect who you are.

The key is training your eye to notice everything you find beautiful as you peruse magazines, wander through museums, explore decorator showcases, and scour flea markets. Then translate what inspires you into unique expressions of your own vision.

Plan your décor around southern values: hospitality, comfort, heritage, romance, and attention to details. Remember to do it the southern way: take your time; don't be in a hurry. Being southern means living at a slower pace, which gives you time to look around and appreciate everything you see.

Take it from this daughter of the South: plant your roots in the rich soil of southern design and you'll reap a generous harvest of genteel elegance with a bit of whimsy and southern-style comfort.

Now go get your "southern" on—and have fun!

Personal Note:

Please let me know how you're doing! You can contact me at:

Kimberly@www.KnottingHillInteriors.com

Get additional inspiration through my blog, "It's So Fabulous!" at *www.KnottingHillInteriors.com*.

*** END ***

ABOUT THE AUTHOR

Talented and much sought after, interior designer Kimberly Grigg creates spectacular dream home interiors throughout the Southeast and beyond. Kimberly began her career at the age of five when she began designing and selling Barbie Dream Homes that she made out of scraps of fabric and her mother's leftover shoe boxes!

Kimberly is increasingly celebrated in the media for her noteworthy high-profile accomplishments, such as the renovation of the world-famous historic Pine Lakes Country Club. Her designs have been featured in select regional magazines.

Kimberly has won Best Interior Designer of the Year awards for the past five years. She has also won the Grand Strand Parade of Homes annual competition. In addition, she founded the City of Myrtle Beach's prestigious annual Tour of Homes. She is also a regular "Style Broker" on the local ABC TV affiliate.

Adored by her rather large and diverse clientele, Kimberly has created a process for design where she combines comfort and livability with elegance and beauty. Her motto: "Live Beautifully, no matter what your station in life."

Kimberly's popular, fun-to-browse retail store, Knotting Hill Fabrics, Gifts & Interiors, is an extension of her design process and philosophy. It is layered with surprising and unique accents for the home and personal adornment.

Kimberly earned a business degree with an emphasis in interior design at Winthrop College. She resides in Myrtle Beach, South Carolina, with her husband, Roger, six children—blended, adopted, and biological—and an assortment of pets.

Kimberly's blog *It's So Fabulous!* has won her many fans at www.knottinghillinteriors.com.